About the Author

Joan Crory was born in London in 1939.

Having worked as a primary school teacher, Joan and her husband George moved to France in 1984 to work as church planters.

The couple currently reside in Northern Ireland and have three children, seven grandchildren and a great-grandson.

In 2014 Joan graduated from university with a B.Th. She hopes her writing will help share the reality of the Christian faith.

Take a Moment is her fourth book.

Dedication

To my husband, George, who has always encouraged me to write.

Joan Crory

TAKE A MOMENT

AUSTIN MACAULEY
PUBLISHERS LTD.

Copyright © Joan Crory (2015)

The right of Joan Crory to be identified as author of this work has been asserted by her in accordance with section 77 and 78 of the Copyright, Designs and Patents Act 1988.

All rights reserved. No part of this publication may be reproduced, stored in a retrieval system, or transmitted in any form or by any means, electronic, mechanical, photocopying, recording, or otherwise, without the prior permission of the publishers.

Any person who commits any unauthorized act in relation to this publication may be liable to criminal prosecution and civil claims for damages.

A CIP catalogue record for this title is available from the British Library.

ISBN 9781785541261 (Paperback)
ISBN 9781785541278 (Hardback)

www.austinmacauley.com

First Published (2015)
Austin Macauley Publishers Ltd.
25 Canada Square
Canary Wharf
London
E14 5LQ

Cover and illustrations by Tom Haynes.

Printed and bound in Great Britain

Acknowledgments

I would like to thank Tom Haynes who, as Production Coordinator at Austin Macauley, has been helpful and encouraging throughout the whole process. I have been included and consulted at every stage and have appreciated the meticulous attention paid to every detail of getting Take a Moment to the bookshelves.
For your helpful and friendly attention Tom, thank you!

A Little Bird Told Me

You are more valuable to Him than many birds. – Luke 12:24.

Since moving from the city to a small country town a few years ago, I have to confess to spending a lot of my time watching the birds in our garden. From large, rather fearsome-looking crows to a timid little wren who visits us occasionally, we have quite a few different species flying in and out every day. Our garden backs on to the local park and sometimes we have as many as five squirrels chasing each other along the garden fence and more often than not, commandeering the birdhouse for ages and repelling all boarders!

I just love watching them all and am endlessly entertained by their antics. There is infinite variety and interest to be found in half an hour's bird watching – so much more attractive than the household chores clamouring for my attention! As I sit at the window, I remind myself that God sees every sparrow that falls, and I find it amazing that the great creator of the world is aware of what happens to even the smallest of His creatures.

I love the Psalms where David is musing on the world of nature around him and talks about the wild animals seeking their food from God, who said, 'The cattle on a thousand hills are Mine.' God is vitally concerned with His creation, and we are included in that.

Have you heard this little poem? –

"Said the robin to the sparrow, 'I should dearly like to know why these anxious human beings rush about and worry so.'
"Said the sparrow to the robin, 'Friend, I think that it must be That they have no Heavenly Father, such as cares for you and me'."

There's truth in that!

All Your Need

Whatever your need, God can meet it:
if you're weak, he'll make you strong,
if you're anxious, he'll give you peace of heart
and patience when things go wrong.
He'll lift your heavy burdens
if you cast all your care on Him.
He'll give you courage when days are dark,
and light when the way grows dim.

God's Supply

Our God has untold riches
so why should we feel poor?
Why should we be complaining
and wishing we had more?
He's promised to supply our need,
to keep us day by day,
we're held within His powerful hand
He guides us on our way.
And when we're tired and lonely
and no-one seems to care,
that still, small voice within our heart
reminds us He is there.

Count Your Blessings

It is good to give thanks to the Lord. – Ps.92:1

In this age of computers, it's possible to find all sorts of interesting things on the internet. Here's a little gem:

'If you own just one Bible, you are abundantly blessed. One third of the world doesn't have access to even one.

If you woke this morning with more health than illness, you are more blessed than the million who won't survive the week.

If you have never experienced the danger of battle, the loneliness of imprisonment, the agony of torture or the pangs of starvation, you are ahead of 500 million people around the world.

If you attend a church meeting without the fear of harassment, arrest, torture or death, you are more blessed than almost three billion people in the world.

If you have food in your refrigerator, clothes on your back, and a roof over your head and a place to sleep, you are richer than 75% of the world.

If you have money in the bank, in your wallet, and spare change in a dish somewhere, you are among the top 8% of the world's wealthy.

If you can hold up your head and smile and are truly thankful, you are blessed because the majority can, but most don't.'

(From website peggiesplace.com)

Reading that makes our complaints slide into insignificance, doesn't it? Let's go into this day, enjoying the good life we have and let's spare a thought – and a prayer – for those who are far less fortunate than we are.

Fear Not

Fear not when you cannot see any way out
of the darkness that gathers around you;
God's hand reaches out through the dark cloud above,
His care and His love still surround you.

Stand firm – God has led you to this place today,
you've trusted Him so far to guide you.
And let nothing sidetrack you out of His way,
He's promised to walk there beside you.

Be still – through the darkness we hear His calm word,
the storm often drowns what He's saying.
It is in the silence God's voice can be heard,
stop worrying now and start praying.

Go forward – and see what your Father has planned,
your doubts and your fears all confessing.
He holds the solution right there in His hands,
He'll show you the pathway to blessing.

God is in Control

Be still, and know that I am God. – Ps.46:10.

In the Bible we find a dramatic story in Exodus 14. After 300 years of slavery in Egypt, Moses was at last leading the people of Israel out of the country and on to the Promised Land. They hadn't been long gone before Pharaoh decided it had all been a big mistake – he was losing an enormous workforce, so he gathered his troops, and they set out in their chariots in hot pursuit. The Israelites, in their journey, found themselves faced with the Red Sea in front of them, and looking back they saw their pursuers in the distance. But there was no way of escape. Their situation was desperate. What should they do?

How did they come to be in such a position? God had brought them there! They had done what He had told them and it looked as if everything had gone wrong.

Sometimes that happens.

If you find yourself in difficulties even though you are doing what you believe is what God wants you to do, take heart from this story.

Moses tells the people to do three things:

Fear not – God is with you: trust Him.

Stand firm – don't rush around in a panic.

Be still – a hard thing to do when things seem to be out of control.

And what happened? The people saw that God had the situation well in hand – Moses raised his rod over the sea, the waters receded, and the people passed through on dry land!

Not only that, but when their enemies tried to do the same, the waters rolled back and they all perished. This certainly wasn't a solution they could ever have envisaged; they could do nothing to help themselves, but God was in control.

He knows the way out of your black tunnel, although He might keep you waiting until the very last minute before He brings you out! That's where faith comes in.

Help Me Lord!

I NEED Your hand to lead me, I need light on my way;
I can see only darkness and I fear the coming day.
My world has all been shattered, my faith can't seem to stand.
I've just no more resources. Lord, give me Your hand!

I've often talked to others of Your love and boundless care,
I've said that in their darkest hour they still might find You there.
And now my day has turned to night, I cannot find the way.
I'm almost tempted to despair – Oh, strengthen me, I pray!

I cannot even try to pray and Lord, You seem unreal.
And yet I know faith rests on facts, not on the way I feel.
Lord, be my shelter in the storm, my rock and my high tower;
give me Your peace within my heart and guide in this dark hour.

Help me to say, as Jesus did, 'Lord, not my will, but Thine.'
I cannot understand Your plan or see Your wise design.
Give me a glimpse of Your great love, let me Your glory see,
so faith shall triumph through despair, doubt end in victory.

Loneliness

They all forsook Him, and fled. – Mark 14:50.

I wonder if this is your problem today? Nobody calls to see you, nobody seeks your company, nobody tells you their secrets, and nobody gives you a hug. Nobody loves you. It is very sad to be in such a situation; it saps our energy and makes us feel that life really isn't worth living.

Loneliness was never in God's plan for His world. He knew that human beings need each other and that a loving family is one of the best things that life can give to us. The amazing thing is that when God sent His Son into our world, He too knew what loneliness was. Let's think about that for a minute.

In spite of all the wonderful miracles Jesus did, the ordinary people turned against Him; they said He was mad, they tried to stone Him, and in the end they were yelling for His crucifixion. His own human family were cruel to Him; the Bible tells us they said He was out of His mind!

But, of course, He still had a circle of really close friends ... didn't He? Well, one of them betrayed Him to His enemies, and one of His very best friends denied that he had ever known Him. How's that for friendship? But there were others in that close group. What about them? The Bible tells us: *'They all forsook Him and fled.'*

That was pretty awful, wasn't it? Have your family turned away from you? Have your friends disappeared? Jesus knows how you feel: it happened to Him, too. But the very worst thing that must have hurt Him more than all the rest was that even God deserted Him. Do you remember how He cried out in anguish on the cross: 'My God, my God, why have You forsaken Me?' Why did that happen? It was because Jesus took on Himself all the sins of the world and God could not look on Him as He carried your sins and mine. God had to turn His back on sin.

Let me tell you something. No matter how much other people may have hurt you, no matter how unkind even your own family may have been to you, you will never be forsaken by God. He has promised that if we have faith in Him, He will never, ever leave us or abandon us.

I don't know your particular circumstances, but maybe there is something you can do to change your situation. Sometimes loneliness can be the result of our own timidity or reluctance to reach out to others. If that describes you, why not make the effort to get to know someone in your street, you might find that they are looking for a friend, too. Or, better still, find a friendly church nearby and become part of their family. But whatever you do, know for sure that God is there and He cares about your life. Remember you can never say He doesn't know what it's like – He does!

My Quiet Time

Lord, life is so busy, it's hard to find time
just to sit down and quietly pray.
But I've proved so often that nothing seems right
if I haven't met You at the start of the day.

I need to find grace for the trials I shall meet
and the problems I know will be there.
I need to remember Your goodness to me
all your love and Your patience and unfailing care.

And when, through Your Word, You have spoken to me
and taught me the things I should know,
my spirit grows stronger, my faith is renewed
and I'm willing to serve You wherever I go.

So help me, dear Lord, now to keep my resolve
to meet with You early each day.
Cleanse my life of its sin, give me joy in my heart,
and help me, with love, to show others Your way.

Regret?

As I look into the Saviour's face
and His eyes of love I see,
will my heart be ashamed as I see revealed
my sin and apathy?

Will I grieve as I think of the wasted years,
and the opportunities lost;
as I see how much my Saviour cared
and my redemption's cost?

No limit was placed on His love for me,
and He paid the price complete;
and my heart will break for my lack of love
as I kneel in tears at His feet.

Day by day let me look at Your cross, dear Lord,
as You died there alone for me.
And myself and my interests will fade away
as Your love alone I see.

Remember

May the words of my mouth and the thoughts of my heart be pleasing to You, O God. – Ps.19:14.

We all enjoy reminiscing, thinking of things that have happened in the past and being reminded of people we have met. I recently met up with a school friend I hadn't seen for over 40 years, and it was such a thrill to talk over shared experiences, and 'Do you remember...?' cropped up very often in the conversation.

Are you one of those people who always buy a souvenir when on holiday to remind you of happy days? Our house has them, too: a wooden man from Poland, a beautifully carved box from a visit to Oberammergau for their Passion Play, and I also have a little cast-iron dog that used to sit on the mantelpiece in my childhood home. These memories are precious.

But there are also things that we don't like to remember. Are there are events which come back to haunt you now and then; some unkind or cruel remark you made and never apologised for, or something you did that caused a lot of hurt and you have never put it right? It's strange that the things we don't want to remember are often the ones we cannot forget.

Have a look at a verse in Matthew 5:23: 'If you are presenting a sacrifice at the altar in the Temple and you suddenly remember that someone has something against you, leave your sacrifice there at the altar. Go and be reconciled to that person. Then come and offer your sacrifice to God.' Notice it doesn't say, 'You remember that you have something against your brother.' No, it's you who are the culprit here.

Jesus said, 'Go and put things right.' It may involve pocketing your pride and admitting that you were in the wrong, but if you want to be at peace in your heart, then it has to be done.

Let's get rid of our bad memories if it's in our power to do so. Memory can be both a blessing and a curse. Let's ensure that for us it is a blessing.

The Prayer of a Godly Man

Let the peace of God rule in your hearts. Col.3:15.

St. Francis of Assissi is probably most well-known for his love of and rapport with animals. To him they were his brothers and sisters, part of God's creation. But there was far more to him than that. He lived from 1181−1226 and the world he lived in was far removed from our modern age of technology. Indeed, he would have been amazed by mobile phones, air travel, and computers. But St. Francis has left us something very precious: it is a prayer, which is as relevant today as when he first wrote it. It is a prayer which shows his deep understanding of how a true follower of Christ should endeavour to live. Read it carefully; it's worth thinking about.

'Lord, make me an instrument of Thy peace
where there is hatred, let me sow love
where there is injury, pardon; where there is doubt, faith
where there is despair, hope; where there is darkness, light;
where there is sadness, joy.

O Divine Master, grant that I might not seek so much to be consoled, as to console; to be understood, as to understand,
to be loved, as to love.

For it is in giving that we receive; it is in pardoning
that we are pardoned and it is in dying
that we are born to eternal life.
Amen.'

The Real Celebrities

If anyone is in Christ, he is a new creation. – 2 Cor. 5:17.

Over the entrance to Wimbledon's famous Centre Court are written these lines from Kipling's well-loved poem 'IF':

If you can meet with triumph and disaster
And treat those two imposters just the same ....'

Thought-provoking words for tennis players whose aim is always to win!

We live in a society that applauds success and has little time or sympathy for failure. There are magazines devoted to celebrity and to those who have made it to the top. The more money we make, the more we are admired. That's the way of the world.

But it's not God's way. 'Your thoughts are not my thoughts,' says God, 'Neither are your ways My ways.' The Christian way of looking at things is often exactly the opposite of what people regard as 'normal'.

Just one example from the Bible. Paul and Silas are unjustly arrested, beaten and thrown into prison. Their reaction? – They sang praises to God loud enough for all the other prisoners to hear them. And when God sent an earthquake and opened all the doors, instead of taking to their heels, they stayed right where they were and persuaded everyone to do the same! In today's language, they were 'weird'!

Take another example: In the 1950s, five young Americans turned their backs on the possibility of good jobs and lots of money and went to Ecuador as missionaries. They wanted to reach the Aucas, a tribe of head-hunting Indians, with the Gospel. One day they ventured into the Indians' territory – and were slaughtered. 'What a stupid waste of life!' people would say, but because of their death, many others have been inspired to take God's message to the unreached tribes of the world. Not only that, but those Aucas have been reached and their lives changed as God's love flooded in. That's a triumph. These are the real celebrities.

Some years back, there was an oft-quoted verse which said:

'Only one life, 'twill soon be past,
 Only what's done for Jesus will last.'

The story of those five young men is told in Elizabeth Elliott's book 'Through Gates of Splendour'. See if you can find a copy and read it. It's an awe-inspiring read. I recommend it to you.

WHY?

'Why should I tremble and feel discouraged?
Why should I worry at all?
My father's love is new every morning,
and he sees the sparrow fall.

Why should I fear tomorrow's dawning?
Why should I dread the night?
My Father's hand will hold me quite safely,
I'll walk with Him in the light.

Why should I think my prayers aren't effective?
Why should I doubt His word?
My father loves to answer His children
His promise is true – He's the Lord!'

When the Way is Hard

There are times in life that come to us all
when we feel God is far away.
Our days seem to have no meaning at all,
and we feel we just can't pray.

There are times when pain is filling our hearts
and tragedy knocks at the door,
when sorrow's weight is too much to bear
and we just can't take any more.

There are times when even our friends prove false
and we feel we are all alone,
when we search in vain for a kindly hand
and we look for help, but there's none.

We need strength at these times to lift our eyes
up to God who, with loving hand,
leads us through each dark valley until the sun
shines again on the way He has planned.

Which Way

The way into life is narrow and straight,
and not many people go in at that gate.
The broad road is crowded, folk merry and gay,
it's easy and painless to follow that way.
Which is the right way? Which should we choose?
The choice lies before us, to gain or to lose.
The broad way leads on 'til it ends in despair;
so follow the narrow way — Jesus is there.

The Lord of Life

THE Lord of life and glory,
who dwelt in light above,
came down into this darkened world
to show His love.

He healed the sick, the sinful,
He came to save the lost.
He died on Calvary's hill to pay
Redemption's cost.

But death could not contain Him,
He rose in victory.
In triumph now He reigns as King
eternally.

A Father's Choice

God did not spare even His own Son, but gave Him up for us all. – Rom. 8:32.

When the Pastor introduced the visiting speaker, an elderly man walked to the pulpit and told this story:

A father, his son, and his son's friend were sailing off the Pacific coast when a storm overturned their boat, sweeping all of them into the ocean. Grabbing a rescue line, in a split second, the father had to make the most excruciating decision of his life – which boy to throw the rope to, and which boy to sacrifice. He knew his son had accepted Christ and his friend had not. Anguished, the father yelled, "I love you, son!", and threw the rope to his son's friend. By the time he had pulled the boy back to the capsized boat, his son had disappeared beneath the waves. His body was never recovered. The father knew his son would step into eternity with Jesus and could not bear the thought of his friend facing eternity without Christ.

At the end of the service, a teenage boy approached the old man and said, "That's a good story, but what father in his right mind would sacrifice his son's life in the hope that the other boy would become a Christian?"

"You've got the point," the old preacher replied. "It's not realistic. But I'm standing here today to tell you that this story gives me a glimpse of what it was like for God. You see, I was that father, and your Pastor was my son's friend."

'When a train goes through a tunnel and it gets dark, you don't throw away the ticket and jump off. You sit still and trust the engineer.'

—Corrie ten Boom

A Willing Spirit

Let everything that has breath praise the Lord. – Ps.150:6.

In the 1950s, British Methodist minister W. E. Sangster began to notice some uneasiness in his throat and a dragging in his leg. When he went to the doctor he found that he had an incurable disease that caused progressive muscular atrophy. His muscles would gradually waste away, his voice would fail, and he would soon be unable to swallow.

Sangster threw himself into the work in Home Missions, figuring he could still write and he would have even more time to pray. 'Let me stay in the struggle, Lord' he pleaded. 'I don't mind if I can no longer be a general but just give me a regiment to lead.' He wrote articles and books and helped to organise prayer groups throughout England. 'I'm only in the kindergarten of suffering,' he told folk who sympathised with him.

Gradually Sangster's legs became useless. His voice went completely, but he could still hold a pen. On Easter morning, just a few weeks before he died, he wrote a letter to his daughter. In it he said, 'It is terrible to wake up on Easter morning and have no voice to shout, "He is Risen!" but it would be still more terrible to have a voice and not want to shout.'

A New Resolution

Make every effort to live a pure and blameless life. – 2 Peter 3:14.

Do you find New Year resolutions a waste of time? Oh yes, we make them in a burst of enthusiasm: this year I really am going to lose weight, be nice to the neighbours, write a book, and so on, and so on. We start in a flurry of determination and in about a couple of weeks – if we even last that long! – we've given up.

When reading through the Psalms, I discovered that King David made a firm resolution that he didn't give up on, and I think we could well do the same.

In Psalm 101:2, he says, "I will be careful to live a blameless life." It sounds like rather a tall order, doesn't it, but I am sure he meant it. After all, God said he was a man after His own heart. I think David's expressed desire here would be an excellent ambition for all of us – to be the best we can, for God.

Think of Joseph, a young man who was horribly abused by his brothers and sent into slavery in a foreign country. Did he sit in a corner wringing his hands and bemoaning his fate? No, he did not. David's resolution could well have been his: he was careful to live a blameless life, and his master took note. The story tells us: 'When his master saw that the Lord was with him and that the Lord gave him success in everything he did, Joseph found favour in his eyes.' His boss had found a real treasure! Read the rest of the story and discover that Joseph remained true to his faith and followed his ideals through thick and thin, and it wasn't easy. But Joseph could lay his head on a pillow at night with a clear conscience, knowing he had done what was right.

Peace of mind is a precious thing, no regrets for hasty words spoken unthinkingly, or for underhand actions waiting to be discovered. If we endeavour to follow David's example and live a blameless life, we'll be at peace with ourselves at the end of the day and we'll have nothing to reproach ourselves with. Life is too short to waste in regrets. I think a New Resolution is called for.

Blessed Assurance

I know the One in whom I trust. – 2 Tim 1:12.

"Blessed Assurance, Jesus is mine", sang the crowd. Where were they? In a large church somewhere? – No. They were jam-packed in a London tube train!

It was 1954 and Billy Graham's great Harringay Crusade was already into its second month. Every night thousands flocked to hear this young American who preached so authoritatively, beginning every other sentence with "The Bible says ..."

The theme song of the mission was Blessed Assurance and everybody knew it. Travelling up to the meetings three times a week with my mother and sister, we joined in the singing in the tube, and it was thrilling. I was fifteen at the time and had never experienced anything like it. We three sang in the choir. We all loved music and it was the experience of a lifetime to sing with that huge choir, expertly guided by Cliff Barrows.

Night after night we listened to Billy's preaching and my Christian faith was really strengthened in those weeks. I watched the crowds every night and saw hundreds respond to the Gospel's appeal. God was at work and London knew it. To begin with the Press had been very critical of Billy Graham and his American 'methods' but after a while they changed their tune. After all, the Queen had invited him to tea at the palace so she must have approved! His Christian commitment was so obviously genuine and his humility so endearing that he won over even the most hard-bitten newspaper journalists.

The Crusade was a constant subject of conversation and it was so easy to share one's faith with others. It was the Topic of the Day.

The years have rolled by and times have changed. No-one sings hymns on the tube any more. But the need to share our faith is more pressing than ever.

Blessed Assurance – it's an affirmation.

'Preach the Gospel at all times: if you must, use words!'

–St. Augustine

Changing Roles

Those who hope in the Lord will renew their strength. – Isa.41:31.

How often our role in life changes! From schoolgirl (or boy!) to working woman (or man), from a single to a fiancé, to a parent, and then a grandparent. We accept these roles for better or worse and work them out with a greater or lesser degree of anticipation and joy.

But sometimes there have been, or will be, even more traumatic changes thrust upon us. A parent or child becomes ill and we have to give up work and become a carer, or redundancy forces us from being a wage earner to being unemployed; illness hits us or a serious accident and from being an active person we are forced to accept the role of invalid ... the possibilities are endless and frightening. How do we cope when this sort of role change hits us?

In the Bible, Job found himself in this situation; absolutely everything had gone wrong for him, and like us, he questioned God: 'Why does it have to be me? I can't bear it!' Read the Psalms and you'll find David shouting: 'God, where are You in this?' To come up to date, have you read the book 'Joni'? Paralysed in a diving accident at seventeen she takes us step by painful step through her struggle to come to terms with what happened to her. And how hard it was!

How easily we say, when life is simple, 'I trust God to work out His plan for me.' But, and I say it reverently, God may one day 'call our bluff' and let us find out what it means to put our lives completely in His control. No, not vindictively, but tenderly to teach us the inner serenity that comes from finding all we need in Him.

David said to God, 'My times are in Your hands.' Can you honestly say that, too, even when life is at its blackest? That's what the Christian life is all about: living closely with God through thick and thin, and learning the truth of His promise: My grace is sufficient for you.

Think about this:

At my lowest ... God is my HOPE.

At my darkest ... God is my LIGHT.

At my weakest ... God is my STRENGTH.

At my saddest ... God is my COMFORTER.

The truth of these words will only become reality to us if we practise trusting Him in the good times so that when the bad times arrive, we are ready for them, with His help.

Comfort

Be strong and of good courage,
you need never be afraid.
When God is right beside you,
you've no cause to be dismayed.
He will never disappoint you,
He will keep you, make you strong.
He will bring you light in darkness,
in your sorrow you'll find song.
Even when you feel discouraged
and your efforts seem in vain
as you seek to share the Gospel,
He will lift you up again.
He just asks us to be faithful,
put Him first in all we do;
walking worthy of him daily,
and His grace will see us through.
Casting all our care upon Him
we will find His promise true:
just seek first my Father's kingdom,
all you need I'll give to you.

Do What You Can

Serve the Lord with gladness. – Ps.100:2.

Have you ever wished you were as gifted as some of the folk you know? You feel you have no special talents and you quietly envy those that can do all sorts of things that you can't.

Well, let me tell you something: God specially created you the way you are – He likes you like that! He doesn't want you to be a clone of someone else.

Here's some good advice:
'Do what you can, being what you are.
Shine like a glowworm if you can't like a star.
Act like a pulley if you can't like a crane;
Be a wheel-greaser if you can't drive the train.'

There's a Danish proverb which says:
'What you are is God's gift to you,
What you do with yourself is your gift to God.'

God didn't make us all the same – how boring that would be! Serve God in your own way, the best you can. Remember, there's nobody quite like you!

'If God calls you to be a missionary, don't stoop to be a king.'

– Charles Haddon Spurgeon

Don't Be Afraid

With the Lord on my side, I do not fear. – Ps.118:6.

As a little girl, lying in bed, I used to look at a large framed text on the wall facing me. It was Isaiah 43:1:

'Fear not, for I have redeemed thee,
I have called thee by thy name,
Thou art mine.'

I used to read it over and over until I knew it by heart.

Whatever your life is like today, whatever you are facing, be sure that God knows all about it. Perhaps you have a problem that is always there at the back of your mind. Is it family, money, health? If you are God's child, know that He cares for you far more than any loving earthly father.

If you have children, you are familiar with that scared little voice in the night: 'Mummy, I've had a bad dream!' And what do you do? You rush in, put your arms around them and comfort them.

Do you lie awake at night worrying about things? Call out to God and you will find that He is right beside you. He says, in His Word: 'Fear not, for I am with you.' Take that thought with you into this new day.

When you cannot trace His hand, you can trust His heart. Nothing under His control can ever be out of control.

Footprints

One night I had a dream.

I dreamed I was walking across the beach with God and across the sky flashed scenes from my life. For each scene I noticed two sets of footprints in the sand, one belonged to me and the other to God.

When the last scene of my life flashed before us, I looked back at the footprints in the sand. I noticed that at times along the path of life, there was only one set of footprints. I also noticed that it happened at the very lowest and saddest times of my life. This really bothered me and I questioned God about it.

"God, You said that once I decided to follow You, You would walk with me all the way, but I noticed that during the most troublesome times in my life, there is only one set of footprints. I don't understand why, in times when I needed You most, You would leave me."

God replied, "My precious, precious child, I love you and would never, never leave you during your times of trial and suffering. When you see only one set of footprints it was then that I carried you."

Get the Work Done!

The people had a mind to work. – Neh.4:6.

Read Nehemiah chapter three and follow the story of the rebuilding of the walls of Jerusalem. The people had been in exile for years, but now some were returning home, only to find their city in ruins. This story is a wonderful blueprint for any task undertaken by a group of Christians. Look at it:

First of all, they prayed about each step of the work. The Bible uses the word 'dedicated' to describe their prayers. I reckon that means that they committed each job to the Lord. That's a good start.

Next, we find that some people thought this physical work was beneath their dignity and they wouldn't join in. You'll always find people like that – but the work went on regardless. The workers were not discouraged.

Then, we find people who were exactly the opposite. Here were men with very specific gifts and talents, goldsmiths and perfume-makers, who were prepared to forget how talented they were and just get stuck into the work of building the wall – 'Salt of the earth' types.

Each man worked at his own little section of the wall without complaining or envying other workers whose lot seemed easier. They each did the bit that needed doing close to home. And it wasn't just the men who were involved. We're told that Shallum brought his daughters along and they got stuck in, too.

Talk about 'many hands make light work'. I'm sure they sang as they saw the wall gradually take shape. It was a communal effort, doing God's work together.

Isn't that the way to do it?

Getting Old

Be glad for all God is planning for you. – Rom. 12:12.

Asked about the benefits of living to be 100 years old, a centenarian smiled and said, "There's very little peer pressure!" We live in a youth orientated culture and older people can feel useless or redundant. Perhaps you feel like that sometimes, but the Bible has a lot to say about old age.

The book of Proverbs says that old age is a precious time. 'Wisdom will multiply your days and add years to your life.'(Chap.9:11.) And where do we find wisdom? The same chapter tells us: 'Fear of the Lord is the foundation of wisdom.'

Isaiah tells us that God will continue to care for us: 'I will be your God throughout your lifetime – until your hair is white with age.'(Chap.46:4.) Solomon's advice is: 'When people live to be very old, let them rejoice in every day of life.' (Prov.11:8.) Moses even had a strong word to say to the young; 'Stand up in the presence of the elderly, and show respect for the aged.'(Lev.19:32.) Now, that should make you feel better!

Old age doesn't signify uselessness. In the Bible story, Moses became the leader of Israel at 120, and Caleb was conquering giants at 80! But coming a bit closer to our own time, John Wesley was still preaching every day – and travelling around the country on horseback! – aged 88; Rubenstein, at 80+ was giving piano performances and Gladstone became Prime Minister for the fourth time in his 80s.

What age are you? And do you use that as an excuse not to get involved? Just think of this: God hasn't finished with you yet: look around and see, there are still things you can do for Him. Ask your neighbour in for a cuppa, pray for that youngster down the street who is causing such heartache for his mother, go and have a chat with that housebound older person along the road.

Someone has said: God is waiting for you to do what you can.

Then He'll do what you can't!

Giving

May the Lord make your love grow and overflow to each other. – 1 Thess.3:12.

Life is full of Giving. There is *Sacrificial* Giving – the parents who go without in order to pay for their son's university education. There is *Impulse* Giving – we see a documentary about children in Africa, who are Aids orphans, and we write a cheque, or a horror like the tsunami chills our hearts as we sit in comfort in our homes, and we give. There is giving because we have to, or because we want others to notice or just out of habit. There is Public Giving and Private Giving: in fact the reasons for Giving are countless.

But the best sort of giving springs from a heart of love. We have all known the teenager who spends all his money on things for himself – phone cards, football tickets, DVDs, magazines etc. Suddenly, all that changes. He happily spends his money on wildly improbable gifts for a young girl he met at the youth club. Why? – because he's in love and he wants to show it.

I came across this wise saying some time ago:

'You can give without loving

But you can't love without giving.'

That's a profound thought.

Of course, giving doesn't just involve money. It includes our talents, our advice, our practical help and, perhaps the most valuable these days, our time. There are people you meet every day who don't need your money, but they are desperate for someone to talk to. Are you ready to give your time to listen?

Years ago I went through a time of clinical depression. It was a horrible experience, but I am eternally grateful to a friend who was prepared to give me her time. On days when I couldn't face the thought of going out, she would sometimes appear at the door and say, "Come on, coat on! You and I are going for a walk." And out we would go. She never bothered me with questions; she was just there when I needed someone.

Is there somebody who needs your help, whatever that may be? We all have something to give, and if we look around, we'll find plenty of people we can give to. It's so easy to be so wrapped up in our own affairs that we miss what's going on around us. It's time to open our eyes! Paul wrote to encourage the Christians at Corinth and he left them with this thought:

God loves a cheerful giver.

'Do all the good you can
In all the ways you can
To all the people you can
As long as ever you can.'

− John Wesley

'The critic who starts with himself will have no time for outside contracts.'

− Anon.

'The fruit of the Spirit is not excitement or orthodoxy, it is character.'

– G. B. Duncan.

Gladys Aylward

My power works best in your weakness. − 2 Cor. 12:9

Most people have heard of the 'Small Woman'. Some of us are even familiar with her Chinese name, Ai-weh-deh, or 'the Virtuous One'. Thousands became acquainted with her through the film, 'The Inn of the Sixth Happiness'. Her life story has been translated into eleven languages.

What was so special about Gladys Aylward|? Why did she catch the imagination of people all over the world?

The daughter of a London postman, Gladys grew up in the hard days following the First World War. She was placed 'in service' as a parlour maid, but very soon became aware of a growing conviction that God wanted her to serve Him in China.

Hopeless at theology and a failure at examinations, Gladys was asked to leave the China Inland Mission Training Centre and she sadly returned to parlour aiding. On arrival at a new post, disappointed but unswerving from her ambition, she emptied the contents of her purse, two pennies and one halfpenny, on to her well-thumbed Bible and prayed this heartfelt prayer: "Oh, God, here's my Bible! Here's my money! Here's me! Use me, God!" surely this was the secret of her impact; her total dedication to God's service.

Every penny she earned went to swell the hoard to purchase her train ticket to China. She also determined to practise preaching in readiness for the day when she would take the Lord's message to the Chinese. So every available moment found her in Hyde Park earnestly exhorting heedless London crowds to turn to God!

Then, jubilation and excitement – she heard of an elderly lady missionary who refused to retire from China, but who needed a young woman to go out and join her. With awe in her heart, Gladys responded, "That's me!"

On Saturday, 18th |October 1920, she set off with all her baggage: two suitcases, one full of clothes, the other with an odd assortment of foods, a kettle and spirit stove tied firmly to the handle. Having waved goodbye to her family, she watched the English countryside slip past the window, little guessing that it would be twenty years before she would see it again.

For ten weary days she travelled, finally arriving at Siberia to be told that the train would go no further because of the war raging on the Manchurian border. Undaunted, Gladys set off on foot. If God wanted her in China, nothing was going to stop her. Many weeks later, she reached her goal, Yangcheng, high in the Chinese mountains. From then on, her story is well-known. She and old Mrs. Lawson opened the Inn of Eight Happinesses so that muleteers who passed through and heard their stories of Jesus could take the message with them on their journeys. Then, after the old lady's death, Gladys was appointed by the Mandarin to oversee the unbinding of women's feet in the villages, and was thus enabled to travel in safety taking the Gospel message wherever she went. She became interested in the plight of unwanted children after being offered a small girl for nine pence! Most well-known of all her story is how, during the war with Japan, she trekked miles over the mountains with a crowd of children, crossing the enemy lines to take them to safety.

Ai-weh-deh's indomitable spirit remained with her through many hardships and illnesses, and her trust in God was childlike in its simplicity. She died peacefully on 2nd January 1970, a great 'small woman'.

We don't have to be well-educated or clever to be useful to God. Gladys was neither, but her total commitment to do what

God wanted enabled her to do amazing things. "Those that know their God shall be strong and do exploits."

God is With Us

Cast all your anxiety on Him because He cares for you. – 1Pet. 5:7.

Isn't it remarkable how quickly a storm can arise? One minute the sun is shining, the next minute there are black clouds overhead, the wind picks up and the world goes wild.

That is so like life. Things are going well and we have no particular worries. The bang, crash, our world crumbles round us and we're drowning in a sea of troubles. Has that ever happened to you? And did you think: 'Where's God – doesn't He know about this? Why isn't He doing something about it?'

You are not alone in that experience. Even the little band of close friends who walked with Jesus felt like that. Remember the storm on the lake? They'd all got into the boat, Jesus as well, to cross the lake in search of a bit of peace and quiet. The sky was blue, the sea was calm. Some of them were fishermen and really at home on the water. All was well.

Suddenly the wind became squally, the sky darkened, the waves rose, and they found themselves in the grip of a full-blown storm. They did everything they could to reach the safety of the shore, but nothing seemed to have any effect. And where was Jesus? This special friend of theirs, whom they had watched turning water into wine, healing the sick and feeding a huge crowd with one little boy's lunch? He was asleep; seemingly not involved in their problems, as if totally unaware of the terrifying situation they were in.

So they woke Him, "Lord, don't you care that we're all going to drown?" Wrong question! Of course He cared. Had they learnt nothing after all these months of listening to Him and living with Him? And Jesus was disappointed: 'Where's your faith? Don't you realise that if I'm here, you're all safe? Don't you understand that I'm in control?' And to demonstrate the truth of that, he stood up in the prow of the boat with the wind whipping the rain into His face, and spoke those beautiful words: "Peace, be still."

Does God seem to be asleep, unaware of the storm beating down on you? Learn the lesson the disciples had to learn: no matter what it seems like, God is right there with you and, despite what you think, He knows what to do. Turn your worries over to Him. He really does care.

'Freedom is not the right to do as you please

It's the liberty to do as you ought.'

– Anon.

'I asked for Strength ... God gave me difficulties to make me strong.

I asked for Wisdom ... and God gave me problems to solve.

I asked for Prosperity ... and God gave me brain and brawn to work.

I asked for Courage ... and God gave me danger to overcome.

I asked for Favours ... and God gave me opportunities.

I received nothing I wanted ... but everything I needed.

It makes no difference what you believe ... if what you believe makes no difference.

God's Plans

I know the plans I have for you, says the Lord. – Jer. 29:11.

Do you believe God's in control and has a plan for you?
It makes a world of difference if you'll believe it's true.
No worries for the future – the Master leads the way.
All you must do is follow; He'll meet your needs today.
Don't waste your time in worrying about what lies ahead,
Just place your life into His hands,
"I am the way," He said.

This is a page for the 'more mature' reader! Perhaps, like me, you are well past the first flush of youth and have the greater part of your life already behind you. Maybe, at our time of life, we are tempted to think that it's acceptable to sit back and have a well-earned rest and to let the younger ones get on with serving God. After all, we've done our stint, and anyway there can't be anything life changing left for us to do. NOT TRUE!

The verse in Jeremiah tells us that God has plans for us, to prosper us and give us a future and a hope. That can't sit well with the philosophy of sitting back and doing nothing. God doesn't say, "This holds true until you reach sixty-five." Look at some other things He says: "I will instruct you and teach you in the way you should go." – No age limit on that. What about, "In all your ways acknowledge Him and He will direct your paths" – That must mean we're going somewhere. We're expected to be on the move, not sitting still and letting other people get on with it.

Maybe you can't walk as well as you used to, your arthritis prevents you from getting out and your hearing makes you miss what people say. Do you think God doesn't know that? But He has put you where you are so that you can share His love with the folk who are there. Remember that children's hymn we used to sing – 'You in your small corner and I in mine'? It might not be a fast-moving area but it's your special plot.

Just think, now that the family has flown the nest, now that retirement is a reality, and not just something far in the future, you have so much more time on your hands in which to get to know God better. Use your time well and try to be the sort of old person – (Perish the phrase!) – whom people are glad to spend time with. God still has plans for you.

Good Health

The Lord gives His people strength; the Lord blesses them with peace. – Ps. 29:11

As a nation we have, over recent years become very health conscious. Every magazine has a Slimmers' Guide and sheets of exercises to give us that dream figure. We all get caught up in it; we say to the children: "Don't eat that, it'll make you FAT, give you SPOTS, destroy your teeth..." And what about exercise? – the jogging craze, aerobics, keep fit, etc. There are health studios everywhere. And why? Because people are beginning to recognise that a healthy body is a precious possession.

But God created us body, mind and spirit, and we need to be healthy in all these realms. Look at mental health; how many people today are living on anti-depressants! Nervous illness can be caused by all sorts of things and often needs medical treatment, but we know that 'Prevention is better than cure' and for those of us who have a faith in God, there is something we can do to safeguard our minds. God has promised to keep in perfect peace those whose trust in Him is constant and firm. That doesn't mean that no Christian experiences depression; it is a clinical condition that can attack anyone at any time, but constant worrying over problems should not form part of a Christian's outlook on life.

What about spiritual health? Even the most godless person today is aware of the supernatural. Look at the interest in Transcendental Meditation, Yoga, – and the 'stars' in the daily horoscope. People realise there is more to us than just our physical existence. We are created with a God-shaped blank in our hearts which only God can fill. Knowing God in a personal way makes us whole. Yes, we need to take care of our bodies; we need to guard our minds, but most of all, we need to ensure that spiritually we are fit and well.

Great Potential

Be strong and courageous ... for the Lord your God will be with you. Josh. 1:9.

Have you noticed that down through history often staggering changes have been achieved by a single individual? Take a minute and think ... about Florence Nightingale, Gandhi, Martin Luther, and even Adolf Hitler, to name but a few. Each one radically changed the world around them, for good or ill, and yet to begin with they were just ordinary people, like you and me. So what made them special?

Martin Luther King famously said, "I have a dream ..." and that could equally well have been said by each of the people on our list. Each of them was driven by a passionate belief in an ideal which they pursued relentlessly, allowing nothing to get in their way. And their influence spread far beyond their own little circle, and changed the world.

When you were little, did you ever throw a stone into a pond and watch the ripples as they spread in ever-widening circles across the surface of the water? John Donne, the poet, said, "No man is an island", and it is true that the way we live can have repercussions beyond our imaginings. God has created us with an amazing potential to achieve, perhaps not in an earth-shaking fashion, but we can all, in a small way, make the world a better place. There's a verse which says, "The people that know their God shall be strong and *do exploits*." I like that.

Do you want your life to be a force for good in the world? Then, know your God – and He alone knows where that will lead.

How Do You Cope?

My help comes from the Lord. − Ps. 121:2.

There's so many things to worry about
as we live from day-to-day:
will the money last? Are the children safe?
And this pain that won't go away.
And I sit and I fret for I just can't cope
and I don't know what to do.
I seem to have no resources left
and I fear I'll not get through.
And then, in the stillness, God speaks to me:
"My child, I know your care
 in my word I have said that when times are hard,
you'll always find me there.
Can't you trust Me to work out your problems now,
just have faith that I'll see you through."
And God's peace and joy steal into my heart
for His promise is always true.

Life is full of problems, isn't it? Look at prices: every time we go into the supermarket, they are up again. And then there's the expense of school uniforms, and buses and meals for the children. We think we have problems when the children are small: sleepless nights, persistent crying, those mysterious high temperatures which miraculously disappear as soon as the doctor arrives, endless washing, and so on. We feel sure it will be better when they grow older. But is it?

Have you ever stopped to think of the problems young people face these days – teenage drinking, drugs, gangs, and even the programmes on TV are teaching them to reject all the things we were taught to value.

What about health problems? So many people today are becoming mentally ill because they cannot cope with their lives. Some are living in fear – of sectarian violence, of terminal illness, of racial hatred. And life seems to hold little promise for them. Some of us are fortunate not to have to live like that, but even we have anxieties to cope with in our families and our business life. We all meet sorrow, disappointment, and bereavement at some stage in our lives.

Well, how do *you* cope?

There comes a time when we all feel the need of a helping hand outside of ourselves. We consult the doctor, the psychiatrist, the minister, the school, or even the Samaritans. And yet, even with all these 'professionals' somehow the problem still remains ours; we lie awake and worry about it, and it's always there at the back of our minds. We cannot get rid of it.

This very subject is often referred to in the Bible: "Cast your burden upon the Lord and He will sustain you". It doesn't say that God will take the burden away, but when we come to Him with it, we are assured that He will give us the strength to cope. After all, that's really what we want, isn't it?

It is only when we are faced with a big problem that we realise just how helpless we are on our own. The apostle Paul discovered this, and then God told him: "My strength is made perfect in your weakness". It is only when we come to an end of ourselves that God is free to work. If we are feeling strong in ourselves, we often don't feel the need of God. Isn't it sadly true that only when things go wrong, people start to pray. God sent Jesus Christ to this earth so that we could know Him, not just in the bad times but all through our lives, good times and bad.

Do you have problems in your life that you feel you cannot cope with? The Bible says: "Cast all your care on Him, for He cares for you".

Interval

I was glad when they said to me, 'Let us go into the house of the Lord.' −Psalm 122:1

What a relief to get away from all that noise and bustle in the street! Coming through that swing door is like entering another world. How quiet it is in here! This is a lovely old church – a real haven for the weary. I love to come here and have a sit down. There's a real sense of Your presence, Father; it's strange, a sort of 'holy hush'. Maybe it's the legacy of centuries of worship, people having prayed in here for hundreds of years.

I wonder how long it took to build? Just look at those beautiful carvings and all that intricate stonework. I wonder if those craftsmen of long ago felt that they were building to the glory of God, or was it just another job to them? 'Except the Lord build the house, they labour in vain that build it.' So many churches, Lord, are just imposing buildings and You are not honoured inside.

I wouldn't feel comfortable coming here to services every week; I prefer my own little church where there's a real warmth of fellowship and I can sing as enthusiastically as I like without having people turn round and look at me! And yet, in a big church like this one, I feel reverent. Maybe we both have something to teach the other. Lord, let me always be ready to learn from others without diluting those beliefs which I hold dear. Thank you for those who felt that You were worthy of the best and who built this lovely place. Help me to be prepared to give You the best that I am and have.

And now I'll go out again into that blazing sunshine and leave the cool serenity of this church. My feet are rested and my soul feels refreshed. I've enjoyed the peace in here: help me to take Your peace with me as I go back to the daily routine.

'Give according to your income, lest God make your income according to your giving.'

– Peter Marshall

Love Is

Let love be your highest goal. – 1Cor. 14:1.

Inexhaustibly patient
Anticipating a person's needs and trying to meet them
Not minding when someone else has the limelight or popularity
Not anxious to impress
Not wanting to blow your own trumpet
Not aggressive but courteous
Not insisting on your own way
Not touchy or easily rubbed up the wrong way
Not keeping a list of the failings of others
Not gloating over other people's mistakes in order to put yourself in a better light
Trusting that in everything God works for your good
Not shaken even by the worst of storms
Everlasting.

> 'Love does not say, 'Give me', but 'Let me give you.'
>
> – Jill Briscoe

> 'True love is always costly.'
>
> – Billy Graham

Morning Rush

Every good and perfect gift is from above. – James 1:17.

"Wake up, Mummy! Get up quickly, it's snowing!"

Shrill voices and eager hands shook me rudely from my slumbers, precipitating me abruptly into a new day.

"Ooh look, it's really thick! Can we go out in it?"

'What? At this time of the morning?' I groaned, and rolled over. The clock said eight o'clock and it was Saturday. Bang goes my one and only chance for a lie-in, I thought. Why do children have to be quite so enthusiastic about everything, bless them!

I got up and went to the window. Goodness, how white it was! How beautiful everything looked; gone the bins, the crumbling brickwork in the wall, the bare patches in the lawn. All covered by that pure snow blanket. I looked up at the sky. Yes, there was plenty more just waiting to come down. A few small flakes drifted by even as I watched. Just imagine every one of them being a different design. That is incredible; I took a moment to marvel at the wonder of God's creation.

Suddenly, the peace was shattered as two small figures flew out of the back door, whooping and shrieking, scooping up handfuls of snow and throwing it in the air. The neighbours will bless us! I stood and watched their fun for a while. Those are my children; noisy, yes, but healthy and happy and thrilling to every new experience. This is another new day with all its promise, and it has all come from God to us. *Wait* a moment, before I start my day I just need to say thank you.

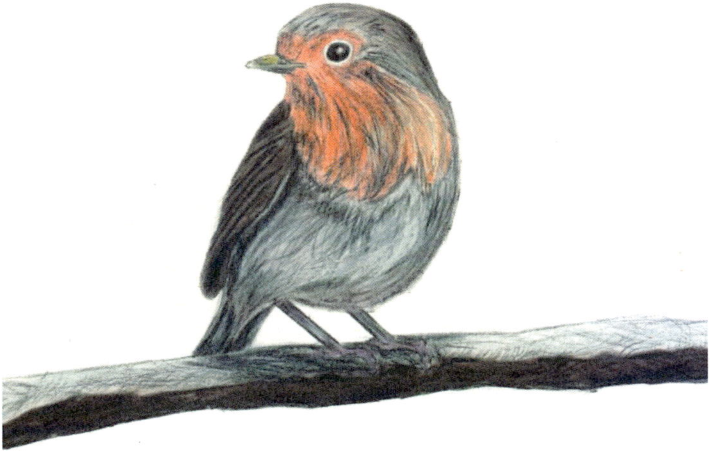

Mother Theresa

Our purpose is to please God, not people. – 1 Thess. 2:4.

If you are kind, people will accuse you of selfish motives –
Be kind, anyway.
The good you do today, most people will forget –
Do good, anyway.
Give the world the best you've got, it may never be enough –
Give your best, anyway.
In the final analysis it's between you and God –
It was never between you and them, anyway.

Resolution

Present your bodies as a living sacrifice. – Rom. 12:1

I would be true
for there are those who trust me;
I would be pure
for there are those who care;
I would be strong
for there is much to suffer
I would be brave
for there is much to dare.

I don't know who wrote these words, but I love the resolve that they reveal. We all have aspirations from time to time to be the best we can be. Maybe after listening to a stirring missionary message we determine to witness to our neighbours and those we meet every day. Perhaps we have read a challenging biography of someone in past years who has been prepared to face hardship and trial in order to take the message of God's love to people who have never heard the Gospel, and we make a resolve to do all we can to serve God where He has put us. Sadly these high ideals tend to fade with the arrival of a new day, and often we do nothing about them.

Jim Elliott, a young man murdered by the Auca Indians of South America, said: 'He is no fool who gives what he cannot keep to gain what he cannot lose,' and his resolve cost him his life.

St. Paul said: 'I keep working towards that day when I will finally be all that Christ Jesus saved me for and wants me to be.'

C. T. Studd also had high ambitions. This was his affirmation: 'If Jesus Christ be God and died for me, then no sacrifice can be too great for me to make for Him.'

Let's follow the example of these 'Giants of Faith'. Let's be the very best we can be in our service for God. When I was young, my school motto was 'Aim High' – simple but profound. I think we do well to adopt it.

'Let God have your life –
He can do more with it than you can.

Ready to go, ready to stay,
ready my place to fill.
Ready for service, lowly or great,
ready to do God's will.

God's work, done in God's way
will never lack God's supply.'

– Hudson Taylor

Stepping Out

I can do everything with the help of Christ who gives me the strength I need. – Phil. 4:13.

You're standing on the brink of something new. The decision has been made – a change of job, moving house, a new relationship, and a business venture. Of course, you have prayed about it and asked the Lord to give you wisdom, and you believe that this is in His plan for you. Why then are you feeling so scared? Surely, it's because you are only too conscious of your own limitations, your tendency to make mistakes, your own lack of sound judgment.

Let's take a Bible illustration. Remember Joshua? Look at the task he had to take on – following in the steps of Israel's great leader, Moses, the Friend of God. How on earth was he going to fill those shoes? How would he know what to do? How gain the respect of those fickle, complaining people?

But that was God's plan for Joshua, as this new move is for you. And God gave him some very good advice. If you are feeling fearful, sit down for a minute and read the story in Joshua chapter one.

Twice God says to him, "Be strong and of good courage". Don't give in to your fears; don't be overcome by your weakness. God works best when we have to rely on Him.

"I will not fail you or forsake you". If you are in God's will, he'll be right there beside you. He won't let you down. As you follow the story, you discover that the result could not have been foretold. The people's response was "All that you have commanded us, we will do." Never in his wildest dreams would Joshua have imagined such co-operation!

Maybe this new venture for you is a bit daunting, humanly speaking. But it's very true that if God calls, He equips. What He asks of us is not that we should be super adequate for the task but that we are willing to step out for Him, believing that He will give us the wherewithal to accomplish it.

So, go on. Take a deep breath and get going. You can do it!

Take a Break

Come with Me by yourselves to a quiet place and get some rest. – Mk. 6:31.

In our busy lives, this is very good advice. We need to 'opt out' every now and then. We need to take time and be still to sort out our thoughts. Not the 'Be still and empty your mind' philosophy but a proper Pause for Thought.

In the Psalms we read, 'Be still and know that I am God'. God wants us to know Him, to realise that He is there and that He is aware of our circumstances.

Stuart Briscoe tells the story of a farmer's wife who was concerned about a young man who was working in her fields. "What do you do in your spare time, John?" she asked. He thought for a while and then replied, "Sometimes I sits and thinks and sometimes I just sits"!

It's hard to find a few minutes to be quiet, there are so many demands upon us, but it is worth the effort. Jesus and His disciples had a hectic schedule, but Jesus knew how important it was to take a break, to get away from the crowds that pursued them wherever they went and just have a quiet time together.

Have you had a hard day? Is life pretty hectic for you? Well, take a break! Count your blessings. Thank God for His goodness to you. Ask for His help. Review your life. Resolve to put wrong things right. Appreciate what you have.

Take a break! It will do you good.

'You may ask me what the cure of this love of self is. There is no question of a cure, the thing must be killed.'

– Francois Fenelon

The Creator God

O Lord, our Lord, the majesty of Your name fills the earth.
Psalm 8:9.

Sunset and evening, the moon through the trees;
wind on the cornfield, the feel of the breeze.
Surf on the beaches, handfuls of snow,
dewdrops on cobwebs, firelight's glow –
God made these.

Colours of Autumn, early spring flowers,
birds in formation, life-giving showers;
days full of sunshine, a friend's loving hug,
puppies and kittens and earth newly-dug:
His handiwork.

God's world is beautiful. Sometimes we get so caught up in the pressures of life that we don't have time, as the poet observed, to 'stand and stare'.

Are you feeling tired and weary? Are the demands of every day getting you down? Just stop for a minute and look at some of the lovely things around you. Even if you are in a busy city, look up. Look at the colours of the sky, and the clouds drifting across the blue or scudding before the wind.

And what about sunsets and sunrise? Take time to stop and appreciate the beauty of it all.

The Psalmist often did that. He marvelled at it all and concluded, "When I consider the heavens ... what is man, that You are mindful of him?" That's where the wonder comes in. Men are planning to send a probe to Pluto; it's going to take *ten years* to get there! Absolutely incredible.

There are still undiscovered mysteries in the universe to be understood one day, but the amazing thing is that the God who created all this magnificence knows all about you and your life and the day-to-day problems you have to face. But that's not all: He not only knows about you, but He cares about you, too.

The beauties of nature which surround us are there to remind us that God exists. And if He could create our world, then He can surely take care of you.

Trusting

Trust in the Lord with all your heart; do not depend on your own understanding. Prov. 3:6.

Many years ago I was talking to my children about their future plans: Which university? Which career? During the course of conversation, I reminded them that the most important factor in any decisions they made was to ask God what He wanted them to do, and trust him to work it out.

Suddenly, like a bolt from the blue, came the thought, "You don't believe that yourself for your own future!" – And it really shook me. We were on the verge of a radical change in our lifestyle: my husband was giving up a good teaching job to go to Bible College, and I was scared. I realised with a shock that it was true – I was *not* trusting God for my future.

For several years I had been teaching remedial classes in the local high school, going over and over the basics until the children grasped them. That day I understood that I was a 'slow learner' in God's school. 'Trust' is a word we are very familiar with but I still hadn't grasped it. We have the impression that 'trusting' means having a warm, comfortable feeling inside us, secure in our Heavenly Father's love. Of course it is that, but it is far, far more.

Has our trust in God ever really cost us anything? Is it the result of battles hard-fought and won? Has it grown out of obedience to what God has said to us? Trust is something we need to *learn* and often that chance only comes through difficulty. Is life tough-going for you at the moment? Take an honest look at yourself and make sure you are not compounding the problem by your lack of trust in God who has promised to meet all our needs. Give Him the chance to do just that – don't stay in the remedial class! He is worthy of our trust: prove it for yourself.

Walking in Darkness

Don't let your hearts be troubled. Trust in God. – John 14:1

A little while ago I became very conscious of a Bible verse that kept cropping up. It was Isaiah 50:10:

'Who is the man that fears the Lord, who walks in darkness and has no light? Let him trust in the name of the Lord his God.'

Being a Christian doesn't save us from bad days or difficult situations. Have you ever felt yourself to be a prisoner, perhaps of a body that doesn't function properly, gossip or injustice, unanswered prayers, loneliness, or circumstances you don't like and cannot change?

In Philippians 4:6, Paul tells us to be thankful IN all situations, not FOR, and he was physically a prisoner in a Roman jail when he wrote his letter. Thank you, God, for being bigger than this situation; thank you that although it's too much for me, nothing is impossible to You. When we get to that point, we will discover that peace will invade our lives. It doesn't change the circumstances, but it does change our perception of them.

A painting competition was held on the theme of 'Peace'. The second prize went to a lovely Lakeland scene, with rolling hills and the evening sun making long shadows across the countryside. But first prize was awarded to a depiction of the rugged Cornish coast in a fierce storm, huge waves crashing on the rocks. But in a cleft of the rock, sitting calmly on her nest, eyes closed, sat a gull, untroubled by the violence around her.

It's not the circumstances that count, but the way we look at them. Isaiah reminds us that God will send us His peace if we are prepared to trust Him when the days are dark.

<u>Hope</u>

There are things in life that happen
that we'll never understand,
but that's because we cannot see
the pathway God has planned.
His wisdom keeps as secret
what the future holds in store;
just one step at a time He'll show –
we couldn't cope with more.
How could we face tomorrow
knowing grief and pain were there?
Enough to have enjoyed today
our Father's loving care.
There's comfort knowing He controls
the way we live, or die,
and nothing happens just by chance
beneath His loving eye.
So praise Him when the days are bright
and trust Him through the pain;
for though today the sky is dark,
the sun will shine again.

What is this Life?

The Lord is the stronghold of my life. – Ps. 27:1

Is it this...?

Shakespeare – ...it is a tale, told by an idiot, full of sound and fury, signifying nothing.

Longfellow – ... Life is but an empty dream.

Samuel Butler – ... Life is one long process of getting tired.

Ernest Hemingway, (who was both rich and famous) – ...I live in a vacuum that is as lonely as a radio when the batteries are dead.

Or is it this ...

There are things in life that happen that we'll never understand,

But that's because we cannot see the pathway God has planned.

His wisdom keeps as secret what the future holds in store,

Just one step at a time He'll show, − we couldn't cope with more. How could we face tomorrow knowing grief and pain were there?

Enough to have today enjoyed our Father's loving care.

There's comfort knowing He controls the way we live or die

And nothing happens just by chance beneath His loving eye.

So praise Him when the days are bright and trust Him through the rain,

For though today the sky is dark, the sun will shine again.

Rick Warren: The greatest tragedy is not death, but life without purpose.

Wise Men Still Seek Him

Wise men from the East came to Jerusalem, saying, "Where is He...?" Matt. 2:2.

Don't you just love Christmas? Crisp, cold days and lighted Christmas trees twinkling in the windows of the houses. The very special joy of singing carols in a candle-lit church. Furtive rustlings in bedrooms with the doors firmly shut and frantic calls of 'Don't come in!' And best of all, the timeless story of the baby in the manger; a story that never loses its appeal no matter how often you hear it.

Have you ever thought about the first people who learned of this amazing event? Take the shepherds, for example. They were poor, despised folk doing one of the most scorned jobs in Israel. Hardly a fit audience for a message from heaven, we would have thought. Nobody 'rated' them, to use a modern phrase. Ah, but God did. Poor as they were, they understood the message they heard and acted on it.

The next group – the Wise Men. What a contrast! They were highly educated, rich, maybe even of royal birth. After all, they seemed to be well-accepted at the palace. They were people of influence and others took note of what they said. They too understood and believed the message and acted on it.

So, what does that teach us? Surely that God is no respecter of persons. Rich or poor, influential or insignificant, God has a message for us. The same message. Have we understood and believed it?

Have you seen the car sticker which says, 'Wise Men still seek Him'? Perhaps it's time to join them.

Be Focussed

Let us strip off every weight that slows us down and let us run with endurance. – Heb. 12:1.

As I write this, the Winter Olympics are in full swing. I'm afraid the housework has often been neglected as I watch the daily TV coverage. I love the skiing: the scenery is gorgeous – those beautiful mountains against what seem to be a permanent blue sky! The speed they go in the downhill, the heart-in-the-mouth risks they take, and the final spurt to get to the finish all make for compulsive viewing.

Most of the athletes have worked hard and practised endlessly in order to gain the privilege of representing their country in their chosen sport. Nothing is too hard for them; nothing can stand in their way. They're in the Olympics for a medal, preferably gold, and they will do anything to achieve their ambition.

The apostle Paul was familiar with athletes. No doubt he had watched the Games in the Arena and seen competitors striving to win the coveted laurel wreath. He makes reference to them in one of his letters and likens the life of a Christian to competing in a race. "Come on," he says. "This is important. Discipline yourselves, and run to win!" Win what? Not a gold medal, or even a silver or bronze, but by achieving a lifestyle that brings honour to God to ultimately hear His words of commendation: "Well done!"

The secret is to be focussed; to set our sights on the ultimate goal and go for it. In Hebrews we're told: 'Get rid of everything that hinders your progress and fix your eyes on Jesus.' That's the secret of success.

Not Just an Earthling

The heavens declare the glory of God. – Psalm 19:1.

Colonel James Irwin walked on the moon. He was the lunar module pilot of the Apollo 15 Mission which left the earth on 26th July 1971. He spent almost 300 hours in space and helped to collect 80kg of moon rock to bring back to earth.

My husband and I met James Irwin when we were working as missionaries in France. We had planted a small evangelical church in a little town on the banks of the River Saone. Just when we were ready to have the official opening, Col. Irwin happened to be in the area, and he graciously agreed to come and do the honours. We put up posters and invited all the town dignitaries, although the general consensus of opinion in the town was that we couldn't possibly be having the real astronaut to come to our humble little building: it would be a cardboard cutout!

However, on the appointed day, all our invited guests turned up and we had a really exciting time. We were struck by the humility of the man. He was quiet and gentle and his Christian commitment was very real. He talked about his experience and drew lessons from his time in space to illustrate the Christian's journey.

He had written a book called 'Plus que de simples terriens', which translates as 'More than just earthlings' and spoke of the Life Beyond, which we can all experience in Christ. After the ceremony, he gave a copy to everyone present and even signed them all. I still have my copy!

Col. Irwin had been a Christian for a long time before going into space, but he said that God had to send him to the moon to make his faith come really alive. The rapturous welcome accorded the astronauts on their tour of New York after the Mission was a shock, and he found it hard to come to terms with 'instant celebrity' but as the limousine drove through the city, he prayed this prayer: "Lord, take my life. Use me as Your servant to reach this thirsty world." From that moment his life was dedicated to God's work. His constant theme was 'More than just Earthlings', sharing with all who listened to him that God's plan is to give us Life Abundant.

None of us is likely to go into space. James Irwin thought it would be the high point of his life, and that nothing would ever surpass that experience but afterwards he said he felt dissatisfied. Several other astronauts have been deeply depressed after their Mission, feeling that life had nothing further for them. James Irwin discovered that the highest satisfaction in life came when he set himself to serve God fully and unreservedly. To the end of his life he found fulfilment in sharing the message that there is more to life than just being an Earthling.

God Knows

The Lord will fulfil His purpose for me. – Ps. 138:8.

> 'The perfect friend is one
> who knows the worst about you
> and loves you just the same.
> There's only One who loves like that
> and Jesus is His name.'

I remember singing that in Sunday School, a whole lifetime ago.

So what does God know? How about this verse for starters:

'The Lord knows them that are His'. You can go through the motions, do all the right things and fool people round you that you are a Christian, but God knows the truth.

He also knows 'the way that I take'. He is fully aware of the path ahead of me and knows perfectly well all the ups and downs that will come my way. Can we not take comfort from that? If our lives are in His hands, then we are safe. Nothing can take Him by surprise.

What else? Psalm 44 tells us that God also knows 'the secrets of the heart'. All our nameless longings and yearnings, all our desires to serve Him and all the little secret things we do for others – no other person may know about them but God sees. On the other hand, God is aware of all the struggles we have with our thought-life: things we wouldn't want anyone to know. He knows and is ready to help us overcome if we will but ask Him.

Lastly, and best of all, He knows 'what we need before we ask Him'; Jesus Himself said that. God is worthy of our trust and knows what is best for us. Let us pray for grace to believe it.

If things are going well, be thankful

If things are not going well, be faithful.

Outer Wrapping

Man looks on the outward appearance but God looks on the heart. −1 Sam. 16:7.

Isn't it a thrill to get a present? Christmas, birthdays, special occasions are all made memorable by the gifts we receive. But even the smallest gift is made even more special if it is beautifully wrapped with pretty paper, ribbon bow or streamers. The trouble is, wrapping can prove deceptive. Sometimes when the wrapping is off, what's inside can be disappointing.

We do it ourselves. We dress up for certain occasions or to impress important people. But how do we look when we're alone and not expecting visitors! Outwardly it's true that 'fine feathers make fine birds' but we all know that nice clothes can hide a critical spirit or unkind attitude.

The Bible has quite a lot to say about Outer Wrapping. James reminds us that we are all impressed by it. He cites the case of the well-dressed man who arrives at your group. His jewellery is impressive and his clothes are definitely 'Designer labelled'. And what do we do? We treat him with deference and give him lots of attention. And how about the slightly scruffy man who follows him in? Well, we more or less ignore him. The Bible says it's not our hairdo or manicure which counts; it's whether we are beautiful on the inside.

Robbie Burns had the right idea:
'O wad some power the giftie give us
To see oorsels as others see us!'

We might get a bit of a shock. But more importantly, how does God see us? He's not impressed by the outer wrapping. He's much more interested in what's on the inside.

The Battle is the Lord's

Lord, You have put Your finger on
the one thing I must do
if I'm to know the peace and joy
of fellowship with You.
Yet, oh it's hard to win the fight,
the battle rages long,
but though I know my will is weak,
praise God, the Lord is strong.
It's He who wins the victory
the power is in His hand,
and when I fear my strength will fail,
I know He'll understand.
I know that I must learn to trust
completely in His power,
believe Him when He says, 'Fear not,
I'm with you every hour.'
I know that on my own I'll fall,
but Christ the Lord is near.
He is the King Omnipotent,
so what have I to fear?